Being Bob

The story of a horse

Written and Photographed by
Suzanne J. Rogers

ISBN: 1475223714
ISBN-13: 9781475223712

Library of Congress Control Number: 2012907401
CreateSpace, North Charleston, SC

Inquiries about this book should be addressed to:
Suzanne J. Rogers
Email: zannyro@yahoo.com
260-449-0990

Acknowledgement:

This book is dedicated to Melvin.
I would like to thank you for allowing me to spend hours and hours with Joe, Jake, Jack, Mac and most of all..Bob.
I will never forget your generosity and I will always be grateful that the gate was always open to me.
Opening that gate, changed my life. The memories of the golden hours spent wandering the pastures with "the boys" will always be a part of my heart.

Bob the horse lived on a farm.

Bob didn't live alone, there were other horses that lived with him.

At night they stayed in a nice warm barn and were cared for by a man who loved them very much.

Every morning the man would feed the horses and then let them go outside.

The herd would spend their day eating hay and grass .

Bob was different, he didn't just stay with the herd all day.

As soon as he had finished his breakfast, he would go explore the pastures and fields to see what was new each day.

One of his favorite things to do was to go check on the birds that sang on the fences.

He never knew what kinds of birds he would see. Every day was different. Every song was different.

As Bob explored the fields, he always hoped he'd find a puddle.

He loved to walk in the mud. He was the messiest horse in the herd.

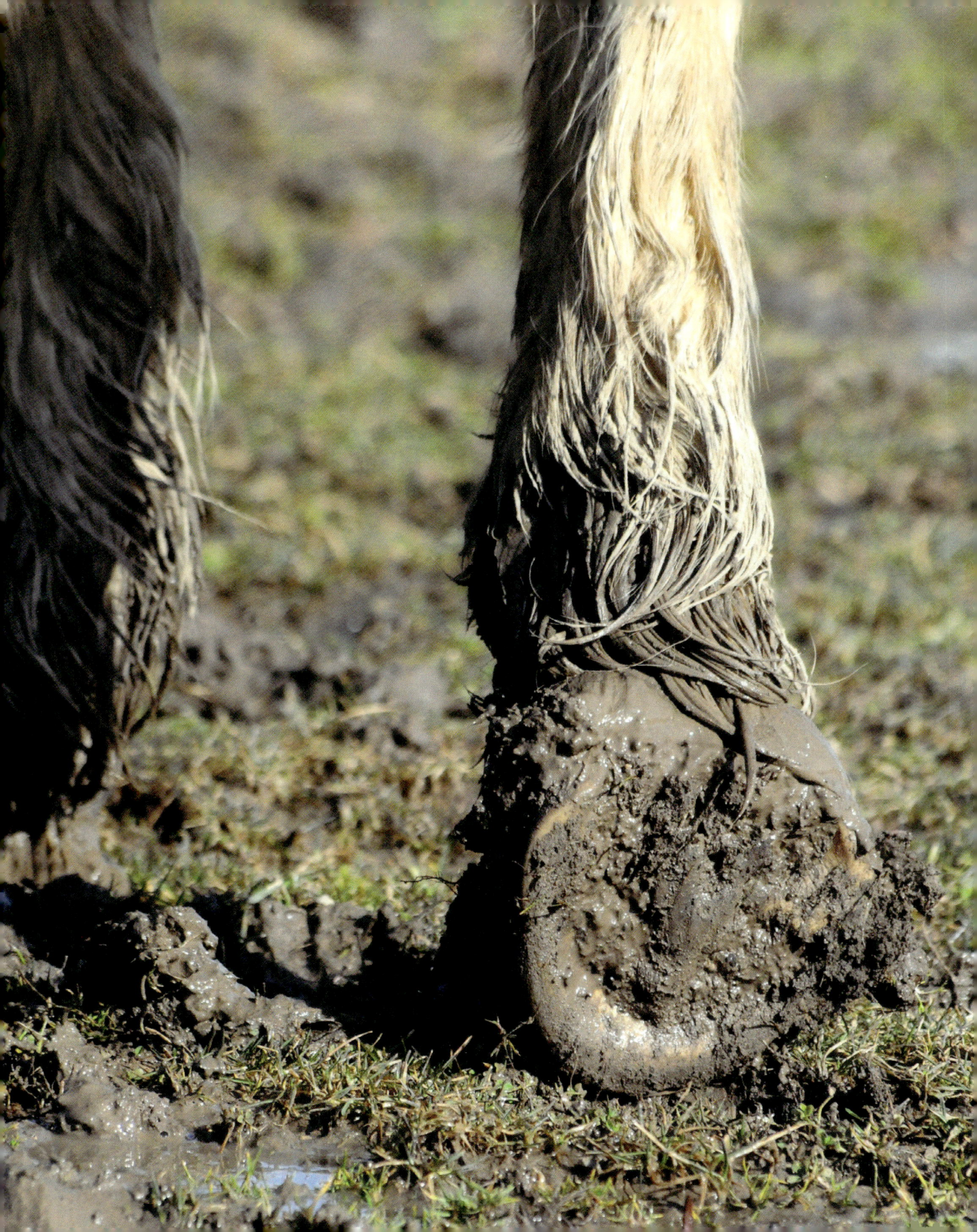

Bob would spend part of his day with his friend Mac. Bob thought Mac was funny and he loved to hear his big horse laugh. They were always doing silly things.

There was only one thing about Bob's life that he wished was different.

He felt like he didn't fit in with the herd. He knew he wasn't like the other horses.

Bob decided that the best way to fit in would be to become more like Joe.

Whatever Joe did, he tried to do.

Joe liked to search for grass growing near the muddy puddles. Bob liked to walk in the puddles but he wasn't so excited about nibbling muddy, dirty, grass.

Wherever Joe was –
Bob tried to be there too.

Bob even tried to make his hair look just like Joe's.

His hair was a little wild, it was never going to look like Joe's.

Joe wasn't very happy with these changes in Bob.

Bob spent all of his time trying to get Joe to like him.

As much as he tried, there were still times when Joe was rude to him and embarrassed him.

After Joe embarrassed him, Bob thought about how hard he had worked to change himself to be like Joe. He knew there had only been one real change and that was that he wasn't very happy anymore.

He felt like he had lost his place in the herd.

Bob got sadder and grumpier and grumpier. One day he was rude to Mac. That wasn't like him..

THAT WAS LIKE JOE!!!

Bob felt bad about himself for being mean. Mac was his FRIEND! He went to find Mac and told him that he was sorry.

Bob realized that he didn't want to spend his time trying to be like Joe.

He had talked to Mac about how he felt, and Mac told him that the other horses liked learning things from Bob. He noticed things that they didn't, they just had never thought to tell Bob that.

Bob thought about all of the things that made him "Bob" and he knew then that he DID fit into the herd. Just like the snowflakes he liked to watch fall from the sky, each horse was different and special in their own way.

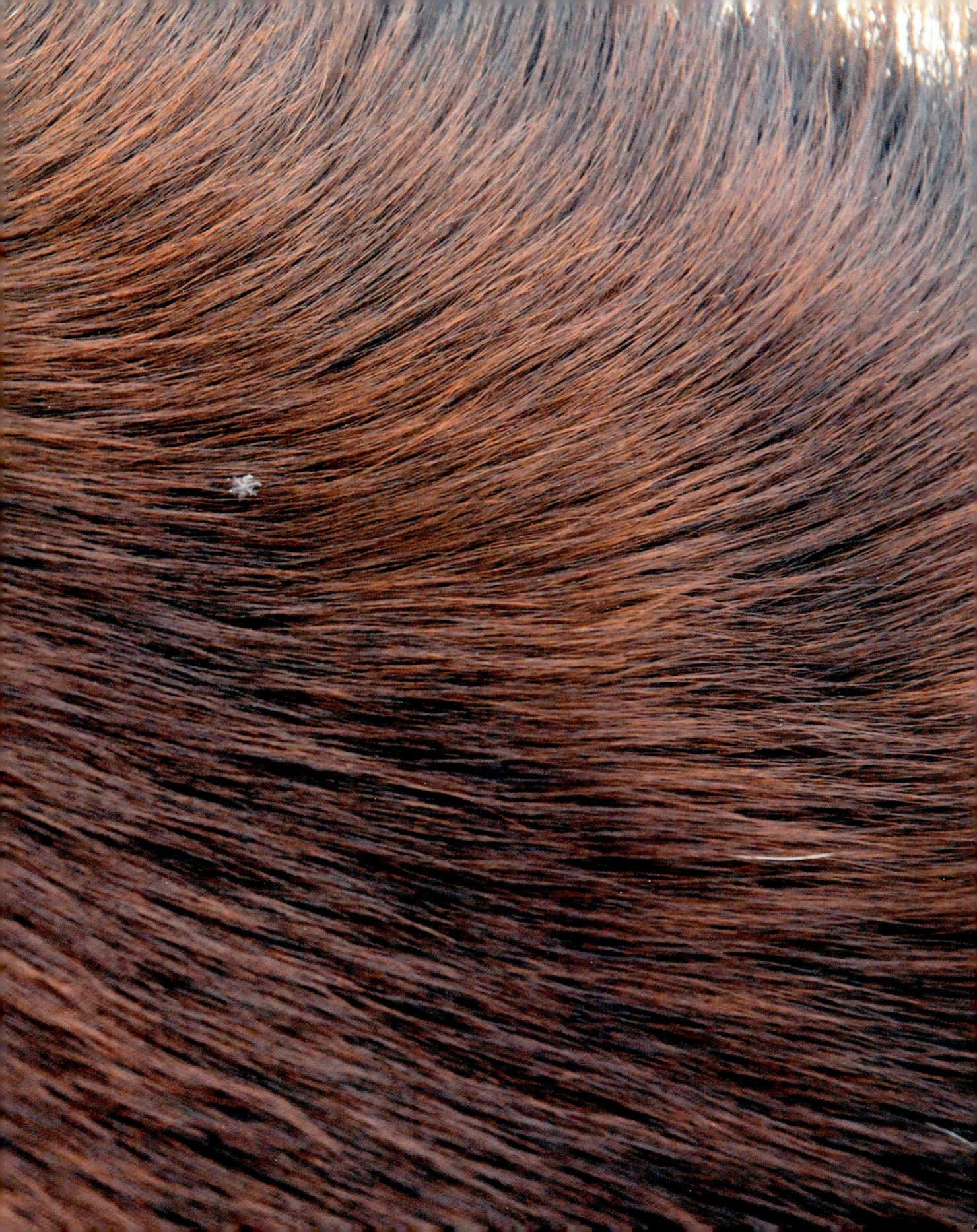

And that's when Bob felt happy again.

Bob decided that he LIKED being the horse that played in the snow with Mac.

He LIKED being the horse that noticed the tiny little flying, buzzing creatures that danced in the air.

He LIKED being the horse who could spend time by himself thinking his own thoughts.

He knew in his heart that it didn't matter so much about fitting in..he knew he'd be fine..

Because he LIKED,

BEING BOB!

The End.